ROCK SOLID PARENTING:

Secrets of an Effective Parent

Rom 12:2,

Lenore

Lenore Lawson Doster, MA, PsyD

This book is dedicated with admiration and appreciation to my husband, Don, who encourages and helps me in so many ways. Without his support, this book would not exist.

TABLE OF CONTENTS

ACKNOWLEDGEMENTS

I want to recognize my high school psychology teacher, Dave Wiedemann, who has supported me since the beginning of my journey, which began in the early 1980's, into understanding the art of the mind and human behavior. Thank you for your ongoing, unconditional regard.

I want to thank my talented and dedicated mentors throughout my clinical psychology master's and doctoral training:

- First, Dr. Glenn Egan, my supervisor at Grady Memorial Day Treatment Center, and Dr. Rick Kilmer and Dr. Linda Buchanan, my supervisors at The Atlanta Center for Eating Disorders, who provided me with terrific practicum training and opportunities to assist individuals and families who were coping with complex circumstances.
- Next, Dr. Malcolm Anderson, Dr. Rebecca Jones and Dr. Nancy Bliwise, who were my final advisors during my doctoral training program at Argosy University. They believed in me and tirelessly

assisted me through my final clinical exams and final
clinical research project.

- Most importantly, my predoctoral psychology
internship training team at the Philhaven Psychiatric
Hospital, especially Dr. Melanie Baer, Dr. Ron Vogt,
Dr. Cary Habegger, Dr. David Tsai, and Dr. Rosa
Cabezas. Thanks to the Philhaven team for their
excellence in clinical training, their masterful ability
to teach the integration of behavioral science and
spirituality, and their wisdom in preparing professionals like myself in the art of being a practical
scientist-practitioner.

Deep appreciation goes to my colleague David Smith,
MDiv, MA, who inspired me to write about many of the
main topics presented in this book and who has supported
me on a weekly basis since he hired me in the Fall of 2003.

A special thank you to all those who volunteered their
time to critique this book, especially, Don Doster, Anita
Stuart, Dr. Allen Hunt, Debbie Beasley, Leigh Anne Spraetz,
MA, Ewell Hardman, MDiv, and some clients who shall
remain anonymous.

I thank our front office staff at The Summit Counseling
Center, Melissa Hackney, Mariana Karrasch, Joanne Allen,
and Kellie Gwaltney, for their uplifting spirits and graceful
service especially the past few months during the final prep-
aration of this book.

And to my main editor, Steven Crane, with *Brains of
Steel*, who is a talented wordsmith.

CHAPTER
1

A SOLID PARENT HAS A PLAN

For the gate is narrow and the way is hard, that leads to life, and those who find it are few. Matthew 7:14

The phone just kept ringing. *Why is no one answering? Is something wrong? Oh, I hope nothing's wrong! My dad always answers the phone. Could this be the day? Oh, I hope today isn't the day!*

It was the day — the day that my father died.

On April 26, 2007, my Dad passed away in his sleep. The reason the phone was ringing was because he wasn't there. The coroner had already picked him up and my mother was at the funeral home with him. I was calling to wish him a Happy Birthday. Dad was going to be 75 the very next day.

I had learned several years ago not to call my Dad on his birthday, as he dreaded those days. So I would call him the day before—smart, huh?

Five years ago, he was diagnosed with congestive heart failure. At the time of this diagnosis, he already had multiple health issues such as adult onset diabetes and severe skin problems. His health had been on a steady decline and most recently, he had been struggling with breathing, circulation, movement and sleeping. So, I knew when there was no answer that something was terribly wrong. I can still feel that eerie feeling—had he died? Unfortunately, my gut instincts were correct, he died just a few short hours before my call.

I am one of 13 kids. In fact, I am the eighth child. I have three brothers and nine sisters. When you come from a family that large, you learn to cherish the moments that you have with your father. And as an adult, I really looked forward to calling my dad. I never knew what to expect. Would he be sweet? Humorous? Sarcastic? If you are a John Wayne fan, then you know my Dad—no nonsense, straight to the point and as honest as they come.

Dad never liked people making a fuss over him, especially on his birthday. So, since my dad was a huge sports fan, I would quietly recognize his birthday by renewing his subscription to *Sports Illustrated*. This was my way of honoring his birthday without his really knowing it. That Thursday, the day that I called, one of my father's wishes came true as he went quietly to our Lord in the night. He would no longer have to endure people fussing over him on his birthday.

I loved my father and had a tremendous amount of respect for him. He was a very interesting, yet simple man. He grew up in an age when tough love and cursing were the norm. Like many from his generation, he had the tough part down. And even though my father was reluctant to share his sweetness, he was one of those who wore his expressions on his face, particularly in his eyes. From a young age, I learned to carefully inspect his kind, hazel eyes, and today, I still miss his clever twinkles, direct stares, and watery sentiments.

Dad was a Western man who was raised in Nebraska and spent his adult years tirelessly tending to his children. Our family lived in the West—first in Nebraska, then in Colorado and finally Montana. These western states really suited his character and interests. He was a very active man, constantly enjoying various hobbies with his friends and his kids, including recreational sports, hunting, fishing, repairing automobiles, visiting neighbors, and community service. He was a man of few words, but spoke with wit, certainty and fearlessness, which captured your attention. At his core, he was a man of steel, sense, and service.

My dad not only had his own style, he also always had a **PLAN!** He was determined to keep us busy, give us kids the necessities of life and provide us with opportunities. I now realize that one of his plans allowed him to have quality time with each of his children on a regular basis. He would organize time with kids by group and by activity. The common interests were: sports, 4-H (especially showing horses), rodeo, hunting, the arts (band, singing, high school theatre), and neighborly functions (sandlot games, cattle drives, or just hanging-out). As a child and teen, I could always bank on the fact that each week my Dad would take me and some of my siblings to participate in or attend the local high school sporting event (especially football or basketball), local rodeo, community cattle drive, or various town happenings. What great fun and adventures we had while forming valuable bonds and needed life skills!

I now realize that it's my responsibility as a parent to continue those things that my father did so well. Also, like most parents, my father never attended a single parenting class. I never saw him reading parenting literature. As my father was nearing retirement I curiously asked him, "Dad, what's kept you going all these years?" He said, "Well, hell, I've got to get up every morning, look at myself in the mirror and like what I see."

It's now my challenge as a parent to awake each morning, look at myself in the mirror, and like what I see. I'm responsible for my parenting plan and at the end of my time, I may be called to attest to this plan. Thus, it's my responsibility to be a competent parent and do whatever it takes to develop sharp parenting skills. If you're reading this book, you're probably also inspecting your parental keenness, and looking to deepen your own skills.

What's your PLAN?

Just a few months before my father's death, I was researching statistics about the self-destructive habits of our girls and boys today. Sadly, I found that the majority of all school suspensions, suicides amongst teenagers and young adults, adolescent drug treatment patients, special education students, juvenile court proceedings, and school shootings have involved boys. When those who perpetrated the school shootings explained their reasons, their responses were either angry or unintelligible, often giving vague reason, like "I don't know", or blaming their actions on peer harassment.

About that same time, I was reading the January 12, 2007 *Newsweek* story, *The Girls Gone Wild Effect,* where it was reported that a recent *Newsweek* poll found that 77% of Americans believe that wild young female stars, such as Paris Hilton, Britney Spears, and Lindsay Lohan have too much influence on today's young girls. The question was raised of whether or not parents are raising their children as what one L.A. mom calls "prostitots." It was asserted that parents clearly are seeing disturbing cultural trends, and yet are more uncertain than ever as to how to fight back.

However, *Newsweek* claimed that despite our increasingly sleazy culture, attentive parents, strong teachers and quality friends are making a difference because teen pregnancy, drinking and drug abuse rates are all decreasing. It was suggested that in many ways it's a great time to be a girl because women are excelling in sports, academics, and the job market.

It was also pointed out that the struggle to impart the right values to our kids is constantly threatened, and is a 24/7 proposition for parents. *Newsweek* writers, Kathleen Deveny, and Raina Kelley said that, "it can be done, but an ancient rule of warfare applies: first, know thy enemy." Do you have a clear plan about how to help your child avoid the harmful traps in this world?

Today, we are inundated with quick advice from a variety of sources, including neighborly opinions, talk shows, the Internet and magazines. So, many parents are deceived into believing that they've heard it all when it comes to parenting. Yet, the majority of adults that I encounter have never participated in one parenting class. Some parents desire to be informed, but are overwhelmed and paralyzed by all of the competing information they are presented with regarding parenting, and they don't know where to start. Many of these parents don't read parenting materials because they don't know which books present the truth and are worth their time—time that's becoming more and more precious and worth protecting.

Most parents I have bumped into in my every day life probably wouldn't be confident, if challenged by a counselor regarding self-rating the quality of their parenting, that they have the tools they need to give themselves an "A" on their parenting report card. In my psychotherapy practice, most of the adults I meet, regardless of whether they are coming to me for personal, career, couple or family issues, raise the issue of parenting concerns. Parents are continually worried about what they need to do to direct their girls and boys in the face of the barrage of negative societal influences.

Thus, the enemy of parents could very well be confusion. But, as the apostle Paul tells us, as adults "we must no longer be children, tossed to and fro and blown about by every wind of doctrine, by people's trickery, by their craftiness in deceitful scheming (Ephesians 4:14)." We must be wise to evil forces that penetrate our minds and hearts. We must be aware that evil forces love to use our best resources, including the TV, Internet, magazines and music, against us.

Every good coach has a game plan. Every business owner has a business plan. Corporations have strategic plans. Colleges and universities have all sorts of operating plans for students, faculty, staff, and facilities. Elementary, middle school and high school teachers have lesson plans. Clearly, every parent needs a good parenting plan!

As parents, we must have a solid set of parenting principles to follow that can be easily remembered. For many years, I've been thinking about the most frequent recommendations I make to parents. These frequently addressed matters are compiled in this book.

> And Jesus said, "Everyone then who hears these words of mine and does them will be like a wise man who built his house upon the rock; and the rain fell, and the floods came, and the winds blew and beat upon that house, but it did not fall, because it had been founded on the rock. And every one who hears these words of mine and does not do them will be like the foolish man who built his house upon the sand; and the rain fell, and the floods came, and the winds blew and beat against that house, and it fell; and great was the fall of it." Matthew 7:24-27

This book addresses many of the matters I encounter most often, and is an overview of what I consider the foundational principles and practices parents need to understand, in order to make the hardest job in the world—parenting—doable and easier.

As you read this book, you will be able to inspect your current parenting resources, and determine if your current set of tools has you equipped for success. You will also be able to add new tools that enable you to improve your parenting acumen and add depth to your parenting plan.

The overall game plan of what God intended for us in parenting is gleaned from scriptures such as what was written in the Book of Timothy: "For God did not give us a spirit of timidity, but a spirit of power, of love and of self-discipline." (2 Timothy 1:7-8). Solid parents **BUILD** a stable foundation for their family. A solid parenting plan requires one to:

- **B** — Better Your Parenting Style
- **U** — Understand Your Family Climate
- **I** — Involve Children in Quality Spiritual Support and Discussions
- **L** — Life Coach
- **D** — Direct Change Effectively and Be Determined to Fight Fairly

This is a book for parents –all parents – for Moms and Dads alike; for biological and adoptive parents; and even the grandparent who has custody of a grandchild, or any surrogate parent whom a child refers to as their mother or father. If you are the stepparent of a child who has two biological parents alive, there is a chapter devoted to blended families, which will be of particular interest to you. As a stepparent, you get a special role: one that can be extremely rewarding.

Let's get busy and further explore the BUILD parenting plan.

CHAPTER
2

THE PARENTING STYLE

"Put on the whole armor of God, that you may be able to stand against the wiles of the devil." Ephesians 6:11

It was one of those nights of surfing the television when I stumbled upon a documentary covering the greatest movies of all times. Arguably, the greatest cinematic series of all times is *Star Wars*. Which movie character had the greatest mask? Of course, the villain Darth Vader! Other great movies include *Superman*, *Spiderman*, and *Batman*. And what do all of these great movies have in common, besides of course the litany of action figures, comics, and other related merchandising they have spawned? Each of them focuses on the classic, universal conflict of "good vs. evil".

Whether we like it or not, most people believe there is an evil force at work in the universe, and although we toy with evil and are fascinated by it, we constantly make efforts to ward off any adversity that comes our way. Being the 8th child of 13 in a Catholic family, I never feared or worried about the Devil. As a child it was engrained in me that the Catholic spirit is stronger than any evil force, and any harm that falls upon us is of our own doing. As a Catholic, I learned many rituals to ward off evil spirits such as making the sign of the cross, holding a rosary, praying while kneeling in front of a crucifix, or wearing a Celtic cross.

Although my Catholic rituals help me be faithful and hopeful in dispelling evil thoughts, behaviors and forces, I've now come to understand the insidious nature of evil. Satan can deceptively sneak up on us and infiltrate us in so many ways. He can become part of our weaknesses and our strengths. One common way he sneaks up on us is through what we consider common knowledge.

As parents, it's now common to believe that effective parenting styles are variable and should be adapted to the child's age, personality and so forth. How many arguments have you observed or participated in which the question was about which parenting style to use with a child under the particular circumstances? How hard or soft should the parent be? Is it parenting by the stick? Or is it a time to solely parent by the carrot?

We've been duped into believing that there are many styles of effective parenting when, in reality, there is only one parenting style that's been associated with academic success, social competence, compassion toward others, self-esteem, self-control, optimism, and perseverance.

Over the past 30 years, Robert Evans, author, educator and psychologist, has researched hundreds of studies on various parenting strategies, and found none with better results in the overall health and academic achievement than what is called the **authoritative parent style**. In Evans' book, *Family Matters: How Schools Can Cope With The Crisis In Childrearing,* he presented his findings on all of the different parenting styles that he researched, and the one style that consistently produced the best results was the authoritative parent style, as it was high on nurture and structure.

Parents say to me that they will do anything for their child. I've come to understand that what parents really mean is that they will do anything for their child that makes sense to them. What generally makes sense to parents is that mothers are the nurturers and fathers are the enforcers. However, it is important for both parents to have the skills to encourage and train the child.

It is important that both parents be equipped to give both high support and high structure. It is the child's responsibility to earn latitude. Each child needs to earn various freedoms, in early years based on age-appropriate abilities and, especially in his teenage years, on good decision making—on a regular basis.

The advantages of what Evans calls the authoritative parenting style is that through this type of rearing, the child develops a strong internal compass and is more likely to connect with peers whose priorities include academic and personal success. These youngsters seem to be able to guide themselves because they have internal wisdom of the way of life and its difficulties and dangers. Kids who do not develop a strong internal guide are more likely to have difficulty interacting socially and to become overly attached to isolating with objects, such as the computer and TV. Kids with compromised internal character are also more apt to demonstrate disordered behavior such as acting out through addictions because they become connected to things such as alcohol, pornography, and illegal drugs.

The Authoritative Parenting Approach:

The authoritative parenting approach is the new and improved version of what is commonly referred to as the tough love approach. It's firmly focused on firmness, fairness, support, and nurturing. But fear not, the love part is certainly not forgotten! Remember, we are called to put on the whole suit of armor not just parts.

The following are some guidelines on how to expand your parenting style, using the principles of the authoritative approach:

Firmness—High firmness means giving age-appropriate choices, encouraging autonomy, and allowing for natural consequences to occur. Firmness requires setting clear boundaries.

Boundaries are rules and guidelines for appropriate behavior across all facets of life. For a child, that would include areas such as bedtime, meal rituals, computer usage, Internet access, and all the areas that affect them until the child launches from high school into young adulthood.

Firmness does not mean being harsh, consistently rigid, dominating or demeaning. Rigid parents have a need to be right about everything. Rigid parents put things in terms of right and wrong and take little time to understand. A dominating presence squelches creativity and initiative. Harsh parents illicit extreme responses of passivity or rebellion from the child. Whereas, firm parents focus on what really matters and their children tend to respect their direction even if they disagree.

Fairness—Fairness means emphasizing both caring and responsibility. Fair parents do not rely on extreme behaviors, such as passively avoiding the child's problems or swinging the other direction by using fear or intimidation through striking or other unproductive verbal means.

Being excessively permissive, agreeable, open, assuring and conforming is referred to as "doormat" parenting. Such parents get confused about what's a parent and what's a buddy. Another extreme version of parenting is the "disengaged parent" who is so distant from his child that there is no monitoring of how the child spends his time and is not adequately involved in the child's life.

The opposite extreme of the permissive parenting is domineering parenting. As a rule of thumb, don't attempt to parent when you're angry because generally this means you're out of control. Don't react impulsively because this translates into thoughtless and rash decisions that can undermine your authority. And, never strike or spank your teens.

Spanking is only effective when used as a last resort. It's generally only used when the child is doing something dangerous. Its effectiveness begins diminishing when the child is seven. If you feel spanking your younger children, ages three to five, is necessary then it must be done rarely and never on the upper body. You must follow-up the spanking with adequate coaching afterwards so the child understands specifically what the proper response is in similar situations he faces in the future. Generally, when spanking is necessary, it only requires few tempered swats on the bottom.

High in fairness means giving lots of "face time;" providing a child with your attentiveness and time. However, this style is not too time-consuming. Appropriate closure is brought to a discussion in a timely manner so as to not undo any parental authority. Effective and fair approaches to closing a discussion and to communicating with your child on a regular basis will be covered in Chapters 6 and 7.

Support—Our opportunities are our path to development, and the lack thereof, our path to destruction. High support involves giving the child the right opportunities and having the child make constructive use of her time.

All parents want to help their children avoid problems like depression, anxiety, social isolation, alcohol abuse, sexual activity, and addiction. To promote healthy qualities in your children such as leadership ability, good social skills, solid character, constructive use of time, an excellent parent captures the moment and focuses on daily activities that will build the child's competence and character.

A well-adjusted child is one that is balanced and exposed over time to a range of activities in the following categories:

- Social—Involvement with friends, family and the community. Activities such as outings with family and friends, community service, and neighborhood involvement.
- Intellectual—Expanding one's skills. Activities such as home repair, crafts, reading (a balance of fun and healthy).
- Spiritual—Involvement in community religious organizations and worship.
- Physical—Being active through enjoyable sports and recreation.
- Emotional—Expanding one's inner self. Involvement in the arts, with animals, or nature.

How do you accomplish involving your child in all of the above without burning them, and yourself, out? Let me provide a simple formula for activities outside the home: Have your child involved in two to three activities a week. Generally one activity is too few and four activities are too much. Rotate the type of activities over the course of a year as the seasons change. For example, in the fall you might want the child to participate in a fall sport, a club (community group, co-curricular school program or school organization), music lessons, and church youth group. This would involve careful coordination. You could do things in a manner such as avoid scheduling the music lessons the week of the club events. Or, arrangements such as scheduling music lessons less during the time the sports league is operating and more after the sport is completed. In the winter and spring, the child might continue the youth group and club, but rotate to new sports and pick-up periodic community service projects. In the summer, the child might want to take a break from sports and youth group, so it's an ideal time to enrich the child's life by involving him in camps, jobs or mission work in the intellectual and emotional areas listed above.

When it comes to constructive use of time at home, there are some general guidelines to follow (see www.search-institute.org/assets/individual/time.html). For elementary and middle school children, it is recommended that they spend some time most days per week engaged in activities such as reading for pleasure, doing some independent high quality activities, and having high quality interaction with parents. Please note that "high quality" means actively participating in engaging, interactive activities, not simply watching TV or playing video games. For your teens recommendations include: spending three or more hours per week reading or participating in the arts, spending some time most days per week in high quality interaction with parents, and limiting time out with friends doing "nothing special" to two or fewer nights per week.

Nurturance—High nurturance involves allowing the child to share his or her perspective, while the parent engages in active listening and solid mentoring. Loving interactions with your child require "life coaching," which will be reviewed in chapter 5. And solid mentoring involves providing a thriving family climate, which is covered in the next chapter.

When you are focused on firmness, fairness, support, and nurturance, you are well on your way to creating every opportunity for your child to be healthy — a healthy child that is caring, competent, socially effective, constructive (with time at home, school and personal time) and responsible.

CHAPTER
3

A THRIVING FAMILY CLIMATE

You will know them by their fruits: "The fruit of the Spirit is love, joy, peace, patience, kindness, generosity, faithfulness, gentleness, and self-control. There is no law against such things." Galatians 5:22-23

To others, someone with severe anorexia looks emaciated; the skeletal appearance of someone starving such as a concentration camp survivor, prisoner of war or third world victim of malnutrition. However, the self-perception of an anorexic person is that she is obese. Certainly, this defies all logical sense. It's baffling to think that people could train their minds to think such distorted thoughts.

There is no reasoning with someone who is in the throes of a severe mental illness such as anorexia: but such is the work for professional therapists. These individuals' distortion of reality is similar to what we would see in the "funny mirrors", also known as novelty mirrors, commonly found at an amusement parks or fairs.

When we see ourselves in a novelty mirror, we know it's not reality. Similarly, most parents have an idea when they are making a mistake with their child. Yet, knowing what to do instead isn't so clear, so parents continue their old habits. Unfortunately, we tend to make automatic parenting choices that don't serve us well simply because we aren't aware of ways to critique and correct our interactions with our family members.

Just as anorexics once saw themselves in an undistorted body type, before they became brainwashed by our societal obsession with thinness, we as parents also can get on the slippery slope to mind distortion. We can easily see this distortion in chronically impaired parents, those dealing with issues ranging from complete neglect to substance impairment to abuse. But, we too can gradually fall into ineffective parenting traps before we know it. One snare to avoid is an unhealthy family climate that fosters personal and relational impairment.

The following chart shows examples of the signs of a thriving family climate versus a detrimental one. Use the checklist below and give your first response to how you believe your family is the majority of the time. This checklist will allow you to begin to take stock of your current family climate. I would suggest that every few months you reevaluate your family climate to see if any of your family members have fallen into any unpleasant or harmful patterns.

Sample Characteristics of a
Thriving Family vs. Detrimental Family

x	Thriving Family	x	Detrimental Family
	Honesty		Lying
	Hope		Pessimism
	Responsibility		Blame
	Adequate Self-Care		Inadequate Self-Care (extremes such as severe obesity, sloth, emaciation, malnourishment, binge eating)
	Flexibility		Compulsion, Rigidity
	Regular Activities Together		Disconnection
	Weekly Community Involvement		Social Withdrawal, Isolation

x	Thriving Family	x	Detrimental Family
	Grace		Shaming (to dishonor, humiliate or disgrace)
	Humility		Unbridled Pride, Arrogance
	Support, Pleasantness		Competition, Rivalry
	Appropriate Humor		Excessive Seriousness
	Balanced Schedules		Hectic Lives, Chaos
	Parents Are Fair With Their Availability		Parents Are Overscheduled with activities outside the home or are excessive with their "screen-time" (such as cell phone use, computer use, gaming, etc.)
	Regular, pleasant meals together		Irregular, Chaotic meals
	Compassion		Uncaring

x	Thriving Family	x	Detrimental Family
	Competent Conflict Resolution – balanced with goodness and fairness		Enmity, Hatred, Hostility
	Respect		Disregard
	Regard for others on a deeper level, appreciation for a range of character qualities		Appearance Oriented, Competitive with Others, Superficial
	Firmness and fairness		Demeaning
	Kindness		Jealousy, Competition
	Caring		Indifference
	Sharing		Withholding
	Assertiveness, Speaking the truth in love		Ongoing anger and/ or resentment
	Considerate Requests		Dominating, Bullying, Controlling
	Engaged, Firm		Enabling, Passive

x	Thriving Family	x	Detrimental Family
	Contained Emotions		Abuse (Emotional, Verbal and/or Physical)
	Contentment, Appreciation		Envy, Discontentment
	Fair Communication		Name calling, yelling and/or cursing
	Peacefulness		Strife
	Internal self-control, Restraint		Substance abuse, addiction (drinking, abuse of illegal substances or prescription medicines, gambling, eating disorders, etc.)
	Parents are Parents and Kids are Kids		Irresponsible Parent, Child in parent role
	Age-appropriate Responsibilities (activities, chores)		Excessive boredom

x	Thriving Family	x	Detrimental Family
	Age-appropriate Opportunities		Indulgence (i.e. gaming with adults on-line, access to uncensored materials/movies, only hanging out with older kids, etc.)
	Freedom within Limits		Freedom without Responsibility
	Healthy Touch and Mature Sexuality		Pornography Allowed, inappropriate boundaries
	Maturity		Emotional Immaturity (volatility, instability)

A few warnings about the detrimental traps listed above:

Warning 1: Avoid damaging errors! Some of the aforementioned categories contain potentially fatal errors. For example, if there are abusive behaviors such as hitting or substance abuse in the family, immediate intervention is required.

Warning 2: Go for an "A" in parenting! What kind of grade does your family environment get? If you placed four check marks in the detrimental column above, your score would be below 90%. Missing more than eight items in the "thriving" column would earn you a healthy rating of less than 80%, or a "C" grade on most academic scales. So, how can you exhibit "A" parent behavior?

The "A" parent prepares for the storms and holds the helm during each family member's trials, challenges, or distress. The "A" parent realizes it's not really a matter of "if" his or her children and family will have to weather serious challenges; it's a matter of "when." What you, each child, and your family as a whole will be like at the end of that storm could range from driftwood, to a pruned evergreen, to a fallen oak, to a healthy cypress. It's each family member's character, and your overall family climate that provides the navigational equipment that each of you will use to weather your individual and collective life storms.

Warning 3: Don't have a cavalier attitude about self destructive habits that can impair brain development! I've noticed that some people are cavalier about the extent to which some of the aforementioned detrimental qualities are really that big of a deal, in terms of their ability to really impair a person's daily functioning. For example, I periodically hear from parents who believe that their children will eventually get exposed to alcohol, drugs, pornography, gambling, or other high risk behaviors, so why not go ahead and let them experiment with them while they're living at home. I hear people claim that it is a parent's job to expose their kids to things such as drinking responsibly so the child will learn to make responsible decisions. These opinions need correction.

Psychological experts have found that the human forebrain continues to develop through young adulthood (early to mid 20s). The forebrain consists of gray matter and its numerous neuropathways. It is the center of intellect and therefore is responsible for executive functions such as impulse control, delayed gratification, planning, reasoning and long-term decision making. Because the teen brain is adaptable to life experiences, adolescents appear more vulnerable than adults to damage that comes from participating in addictive behaviors. And one area that is particularly vulnerable to impairment is the motivational center, which typically means that all the teen's motivation gets funneled into seeking their "substance" of choice. We see teens that dabble with addictive habits, whether it be alcohol, abuse of illegal substances or prescription medicines, gambling, on-line gaming or eating disorders, struggle in numerous areas, including:

- Socially—reduced involvement with quality friends in the community, resisting outings with family and friends, and not contributing to their neighborhood
- Intellectually—having performance problems in school and participating in less quality extracurricular activities (including hobbies, organizations, and reading)
- Spiritually—rebelling against participating in worship and youth programs

- Physically—Underperforming in, losing enjoyment in, or dropping out or sports and recreational activities
- Emotional—becoming less involved in the arts, or with animals, or nature

For decades we've used the term "young adulthood" to describe the period of time between the teenage years and adulthood. It is simply apparent that there is a difference between young adults and adults. Now, you have a neurobiological explanation for the young adult time of life. But, many adults are losing sight of the distinctions between teens, young adults, and adults. It is essential that the parents continue making this distinction and to protect their family from destructive habits.

So, remember that the brain is an organ and it can be damaged! You certainly don't want your child's brain being compromised before it is fully developed. For more information about brain development, parents can start by consulting the National Institute of Mental Health's website.

For parents to enable children to experiment with high risk behaviors is asking them to make adult choices when they are only capable of making short-term child and teen choices. Education without experimentation is the solution.

Warning 4: Come to terms with the reality of many addictive habits! It is easier to comprehend that ingesting drugs, such as cocaine and heroine, alter the brain's chemicals in such a fashion that a person is incapable of solid reasoning, and thus vulnerable to chronic powerlessness over the drug. And although behaviors such as gambling are non-drug addictions, most people understand the powerful potentials for entrapment. But, most people haven't thought about the fact that sex can be as addictive as gambling or drugs.

Addiction specialists today now believe that sex addictions, such as the viewing of pornography, and your broad range of sexual integrity problems, are as entrapping and powerful as a heroine addiction. It's simply hard to fathom that despite the fact that even though no chemical is being used, sexual acting out can pave addictive pathways in the brain that are as out of control as a drug addiction.

Warning 5: Beware of the insidious traps! Some people have fallen into the habit of being extremely appearance-oriented. For example, a high drive for thinness is the norm in this society, yet it is also a precursor to eating disorders such as anorexia, bulimia, and binge eating disorder. Most people are frightened about our growing "overweight" problem in our society. But, what most people don't realize is that our high drive for thinness mentality is distorting our view of what is truly healthy. For example, most people don't know that at less than 85% of one's expected body weight, one begins to be medically compromised and meets at least some of the criteria for a diagnosis of anorexia. So, as a parent it's important to become educated about what true physical health is.

Warning 6: Be on guard for skewed worldly influences! On February 19, 2007 the American Psychological

Association (APA) reported that the proliferation of sexualized images of girls and young women in advertising, merchandising, and media negatively affects girls across a variety of health domains, including:

- Cognitive and Emotional Consequences: Sexualization and objectification undermine a person's confidence in and comfort with her own body, leading to emotional and self-image problems, such as shame and anxiety.
- Mental and Physical Health: Research links sexualization with three of the most common mental health problems diagnosed in girls and women— eating disorders, low self-esteem, and depression or depressed mood.
- Sexual Development: Research suggests that the sexualization of girls has negative consequences on their ability to develop a healthy sexual self-image.

The APA report calls on parents, school officials, media, and all health professionals to be aware of, and on the alert for the potential impact of sexualization on girls and young women. Sexualization was defined as occurring when a person's value comes only from her/his sexual appeal or behavior, to the exclusion of other characteristics, and/or when a person is sexually objectified, i.e., made into a thing for another's sexual use. For more information regarding this APA press release, see www.apa.org/releases/sexualization. html.

As parents, we know what we know from what we have observed, discussed and read. **Who have you been observing? Who have you been talking with? And, what have you been reading?** The brain is much like the body; it is an organ that has to be fed. You can either feed it with healthy, balanced information, or you can feed it with garbage. Before you can coach and train your child, you have to stop and come to grips with how your mind has been programmed.

As adults, we don't get comprehensive evaluations on our parenting skills. We don't have a readily accessible report card providing our child management grade. Clearly, a dependable job, great friends, supportive extended family, good neighborhood, stable income, and assisting your children in obtaining a quality education are the springboards to setting a solid foundation for your child, but these aspects are simply not enough to ensure that the child has the proper foundation in which to develop solid character.

You have to look deeper. You have to determine **who's in control of your family climate—you, your child, or society**? What safeguards do you have in place to keep watch for slight declines in family traits and family members' character qualities that can slowly, rather imperceptibly build to become a major flaw? What boundaries have been established by you in terms of communication and relating?

Unlike adults, children are regularly assessed. In school, students receive pop quizzes, pretests, progress reports, midterms, finals, report cards, tests of basic skills, comps, and the list goes on. But, as parents we often don't have as many creative and automatic ways of seeing how our children are responding to our rearing, and how they are progressing. Looking at the qualities of your family climate will help you watch how your child is being programmed.

Another simple exercise that can help you gain a picture of how your child is functioning psychologically is to imagine for a moment that your child is an automobile. **What's fueling that child?** Is the gas that child's running on something like fear, anger, tenseness, sadness, aloofness, faithfulness, optimism, strength, arrogance, selfishness? If you're child's manner is consistently unpleasant, such as seen in aggressive, sad, violent, withdrawn, unmotivated, or anxious children, it's important to consider seeking professional guidance as soon as possible. As a rule of thumb, it's best to seek guidance within three months of noticing impairment.

Given that children are constantly under the watchful eye of adults, they're often the first focus of the family during stress, and the buck stops there. However, frequently parents do feel guilty about their child's behavior and wonder if somehow they've contributed to their child's struggles. More often than not, parents either ruminate over the child's struggles and are befuddled about the next steps, or sometimes even ask the child if there's something that they did or didn't do as parents that facilitated the downfall. But these strategies rarely foster a healing environment.

What IS helpful, is for you to take stock of your family climate while care is being focused on your child. You can determine if your child's troubling behaviors, such as fears, worries, anger, lethargy, or sadness, are a reflection of, or being enabled to occur, as a result of the family climate. You will learn more about how to correct the troubling interactions and behaviors in your family in chapters 5-7.

CHAPTER
4

SPIRITUALITY

*"Do not be conformed to this world but be trans-
formed by the renewal of your mind, that you may
prove what is the will of God, what is good and
acceptable and perfect." Romans 12:2*

More and more research is being published suggesting
that spirituality has a positive effect on individuals.
Beginning in the late 1980's, researchers such as Pargament
(1988), who is an internationally known psychology professor
at the University of Maryland, explored and quantified the
role various spiritual coping patterns had on mental health
when dealing with negative life events (e.g.illness or death
of a loved one, loss of a job, divorce, personal illness).

By the 1990's, researchers such as Hathaway and
Pargament (1990) reported that "it is not merely how much,
but in what way one is religious that will determine the

implications of religiousness for mental health." Through the 1990's, more and more researchers looked into the spiritual life of Christians and declared that the time had come for the field of psychology to investigate not whether, but how their spirituality makes a difference (Koenig, Pargament & Nielsen, 1998; Pargament et al., 1990).

Pargament and his associates (Pargament et al.,1990 & 1998) studied samples of members of various churches who were exposed to the Oklahoma City Bombing, college students coping with major life stressors, and elderly hospitalized patients coping with serious medical illnesses. They concluded that specific religious coping styles (experiencing God as a supportive partner in problem solving, involvement in religious rituals, religious forgiveness, seeking spiritual support from congregation members and clergy) predict physical and mental health above and beyond the effects of nonreligious forms of coping. Furthermore, these researchers declared that religious coping cannot be "reduced" to nonreligious forms of coping.

The research on the value of spirituality continues by those such as Kenneth Pargament. His recent research addresses how elderly people who struggle with their religious beliefs and hold negative perceptions about their relationships with God and life meaning have an increased risk of death, even after controlling for physical and mental health and demographic characteristics (for a summary of his recent research projects see www.bgsu.edu/organizations.cfdr/about/facultymembers/pargament.html).

Another piece of contemporary research demonstrating the positive effects of religion on child development was a study done by John Bartkowski, a sociologist at Mississippi State University. A summary of this research was posted by Melinda Wenner on April 24, 2007 in a special report to *Live Science* (see www.livescience.com/health/070424_religion_kids.html).

In Bartkowski's research, parents and teachers of more than 16,000 children, most of them first graders, were asked to rate how much self control they believed the kids had, how often they exhibited poor or unhappy behavior, and how well they respected and worked with their peers.

The conclusion of the study was that the children of parents whom regularly attended religious services—especially when both parents did so frequently—and talked with their kids about religion were rated by both parents and teachers as having better self-control, social skills, and approaches to learning than kids with non-religious parents. But, when parents argued frequently about religion, the children were more likely to have problems.

Bartkowski also concluded that religion can hurt if faith is a source of conflict or tension in the family, and that religion can be good for children for three reasons. First, those religious networks provide social support to parents, and this can improve their parenting skills. Bartkowski asserted that children who are brought into such networks, and who hear parental messages reinforced by other adults, may take more to heart the messages that they receive in the home. Second, the types of values and norms that circulate in religious congregations tend to be self-sacrificing and pro-family. Last, religious organizations imbue parenting with sacred meaning and significance.

This type of research is not surprising. In fact, it's exciting! When I look around at the difference I see Christianity making on individuals and communities, it is no mystery to me. I know the immeasurable value of spiritual community support and spiritual upbringing. There is certain guidance, expectations, and power within a spiritual framework for us as parents and for our kids, which is only taught through the Word and worship. Spiritual organizations aren't perfect, but it is readily apparent that overall, they have an ability to boost families.

George Barna, author of *Transforming Children into Spiritual Champions,* provided his perspective on what children need to know to make sense of the world and to begin assisting a child in developing a spiritual worldview. He wrote:

> "From their earliest moments out of the womb, their brains are working furiously trying to analyze the information that is pouring in and demanding interpretation and response. As children grow up, they develop mental categories that make such analysis and interpretation more efficient. **Before they reach junior high, they have developed a worldview.** That life lens enables them to quickly size up a situation and respond in ways that are consistent with what they believe is appropriate. Unfortunately, most Americans develop their worldview by default. In other words, it is essentially learned through unplanned sources."

Barna claimed that if we want to transform our society so that it honors God, we must address the worldview that most young people embrace. He said that they are prone to behavior that is consistent with their beliefs, and their beliefs are the result of their worldview.

Barna began by helping adults understand **the four cornerstones that are required to help children develop a biblical worldview**, which are:

- helping children rely on the Bible as a credible source,
- leading children to have a commanding knowledge of biblical content,
- teaching how biblical content ties to their own life and it provides practical counsel for managing daily happenings, and
- motivating children to have a burning desire and thirst for spiritual guidance.

Barna suggested that for adults to begin to assist children in their spiritual development, they must process the following types of questions with children:

1. Does God exist?
2. What is the character and nature of God?
3. How and why was the world created?
4. What is the nature and purpose of humanity?
5. What happens after we die on earth?
6. What spiritual authorities exist?
7. What is truth?

Before beginning this process, I suggest that you as a parent have a basic level of proficiency using all the tools presented in this book. Otherwise, slow down and consult a professional first. I suggest that you approach your children with the above questions at various developmental phases — preschool, early elementary, upper elementary, early middle school, later middle school, early high school, middle high school — of their lives. If you hear distorted or disturbing responses out of reach for you to correct, consider scheduling a parent management consultation with a clergy member or a spiritual professional counselor as soon as possible.

Most of the time, I'm guessing you'll be able to handle discussing these important questions with your child. For example, not long ago I was teaching my child about Jesus' famous Sermon on the Mount. My son said he had heard of this sermon that Jesus gave on a mountain. I explained to him that it's found in the Bible in the first Book of the New Testament. In fact, it's Matthew 5, 6 and 7. I had my son locate the sections and read one paragraph from each section. After reading the first part of Matthew 7 ("Judge not ...the measure you give will be the measure you get...first take the log out of your own eye, and then you will see clearly to take the speck out of your brother's eye."), I asked him what he thought it meant. He said something like, "I think it means that if you and your friend have a stick in their eye, first take the stick out of your eye so you can see and you'll know how to do (remove) it for them... and wash your hands before you help (the friend)."

I was sort of surprised that this is the way my son processed this information, but then again I wasn't because, after all, he is a fourth grader. I was quickly reminded that fourth graders take things literally, rather than symbolically, because of the level of their brain development. So, I told him that yes that's one way to understand the scripture, but that there's another way to take the scripture.

I informed my son that this scripture is teaching the difference between using good judgment and being judgmental. I used an example of bullying to explain the concept so he might understand. I explained that it wouldn't be good judgment to follow a friend who was bullying another classmate by joining in and calling the other classmate names (i.e. idiot, stupid, or jerk). He agreed that it was clearly a bad idea to join in. So, I continued on, and stated that it would also be incorrect and judgmental to handle the situation by calling his friend a big jerk or some other name. I told him that it would be good judgment to point out to his friend that bullying was a behavior that he wasn't going to do and that he thought it was wrong. My son seemed to get this because he agreed that focusing on the wrong behavior was the best option and what Jesus would prefer rather than calling his friend a name.

Much of the time what we face as parents is something like the above and easily handled if we are creative, practical, and use the set of tools presented throughout this book. As we move to the next chapter, you begin to find even more detailed information about how to coach your child through life's various problems and dilemmas.

CHAPTER
5

BE A SOLID LIFE COACH

Train up a child in the way he should go, and when
he is old he will not depart from it. Proverbs 22:6

It's a hard time for kids and it's a hard time for parents. As parents, we focus on ways to help our children get a good education so they can have a bright future and lifestyle. As parents, we know about the "intelligence quotient" (IQ), and how helpful it is to possess a solid IQ so one can excel academically. But, have you heard about the "master aptitude?"

Daniel Goleman, author of *Emotional Intelligence: Why it can matter more than IQ*, described the master aptitude as the general sense in which an individual channels one's emotions toward a productive end. He argued that when people of high IQ flounder and those of modest IQ do surprisingly well, quite often it is due to emotional intelligence.

Goleman warned us that the consequences of failing to learn the basics of emotional intelligence are increasingly dire. He reported that evidence suggests, for example, that girls who fail to learn to distinguish between the feeling of anxiety and hunger are most at risk for eating disorders, while those who have trouble controlling impulses in the early years are more likely to get pregnant by the end of their teen years. For boys, impulsivity in the early years may foretell a heightened risk of delinquency or violence. And for all children, an inability to handle anxiety and depression increases the likelihood of later abusing drugs or alcohol. Goleman suggested that given these realities, parents need to make the best use of the golden moments they have with their children, taking a purposeful and active role in coaching their children in key human skills like understanding and handling troubling feelings, controlling impulses, and developing empathy.

It's just not enough to lecture your child or scare your child into change through the use of discipline. Parents need to realize that coaching is the hammer in their parenting toolbox. What person managing a household doesn't have a hammer? Even if you have a virtually nonexistent set of tools, or have limited funds, you generally have a hammer!

In 1997, Goleman provided the foreword to John Gottman's *Raising an Emotionally Intelligent Child,* and suggested that Gottman offered a scientifically grounded, eminently practical five step method for parents to give their children this essential tool for life. In my practice, I've remained busy teaching new parents, and reminding experienced ones, about the concept of what Goleman and Gottman call "emotion coaching."

I, however, consider this "life coaching" given the initial push back, especially from fathers, when I've introduced this concept. I've had many fathers hear the word emotion coaching and instantly recoil. They become unreceptive and challenging about whether or not emotion coaching is something that will teach their son to be weak. In reality, according to psychological experts, it is individuals, male and female, who have high emotional IQs that possess a greater chance of overall life success. The essentialness of having a solid emotional IQ was best said by a male master counselor that I once knew, who is now deceased:

"Human beings are creatures with feelings. There is no escaping the feelings, or their effect on both communication and relationships. If I am to be an effective communicator, and if I am to be satisfactorily involved in relationships, it is necessary for me to be in touch with my feelings and to know something of the influence they are having on what is happening to me. My feelings "come through" in my communication. I may try to hide them—and may be remarkably successful in blocking many of them from view. Nonetheless, they significantly influence and affect what happens within me, and between me and any other person with whom I have contact. It is highly desirable to be in touch with emotions if you want to know much about yourself and anyone else. So, as I have discovered, feelings are in me, you and your child anyway. And, they must be reckoned with if the child is to be effective with himself or anyone else." – (Overton, 2000)

So, when directing children to solve their life challenges and problems—whether it be outburst of anger, resistance to chores, performance anxiety, school behavioral problems, peer conflicts, or what have you—the best parental interventions, those that build a capable and resilient child, include life coaching.

Do not let your guidance and limits fall on deaf ears! Truly involve yourself in hearing the child and winning the child's confidence that you are a person he can trust to help him deal effectively with his life. The steps of life coaching that I recommend are easily remembered by thinking of the acronym of **HEARing** your child first.

- **H**—Hear the child's dilemma from the child's perspective. Be aware of the child's experience. Use empathy and clarification.
- **E**—Emotion identification—Encourage emotional competency by helping children verbally label their emotions
- **A**—Affirm—validate before problem solving.
- **R**—Review options and set limits while helping the child problem solve.

Hearing a child's dilemma is easier said than done! You must understand the problem from the child's perspective, which is especially difficult the younger the child. For example, an elementary school child reports that, "I had the most horrible day of my life because I got in trouble with my teacher for something that wasn't my fault, I was called a name by my friend, and I had to eat a lunch that was awful and left me starving the rest of the day!" Many adults just blow this off and tell the child something like, "tomorrow will be a better day...mind your teacher...and don't let the bully bother you until the bully does something big like hit you...if the bully hits you, you have my permission to not take it and hit them back..."

Keep in mind that the above example is one of not really taking time to understand the child's perspective of the situation. The above problems are likely as important to an elementary age child as the problem of not having the funds to be able to pay the next month's electricity bill on time would be to an adult!

You must allow for understanding and empathy. Understanding starts with asking the **who, what, when, where, and why** questions. Pretend that you're a video camera, and later will be able to play back for others, such as your spouse, exactly what the situation was like for the child. Or, pretend that you're a journalist gathering information that you will later incorporate into your column about everyday life for children the same age as your child (a column called, "A Day in the life of..."), which will be of interest to parents with kids that age.

Empathy is not sympathy. It's not feeling sorry for the person. It's having the capacity for compassion. It's being sensitive to another, and able to vicariously experience the feelings, thoughts, and experiences of another. It's also not being absorbed with yourself by saying, "Oh this reminds me of when I was a child…and this is how I handled the situation…" You may remember a situation when you were a child to help you have compassion, but stay focused on the child's dilemma from the child's perspective, not your's.

Emotion identification is another difficult, but essential step in life coaching. This is the most frequently skipped step, but remember, to be effective with oneself and anyone else, a necessary step!

When helping the child verbally label her emotions, keep it simple. Keep in mind that, simply put, emotions fall into two categories: there are pleasant emotions and unpleasant emotions. Also keep in mind that you don't have to be exactly correct when identifying a child's feelings about a situation. The best strategy to use with kids, and adults for that matter, is to guess at what the person may be feeling. For example, you would say something like: "I guess you're disappointed in yourself for getting in trouble with your teacher;" or, "I guess you feel helpless about getting the bully to stop bothering you;" or, "I guess you felt surprised and hurt when your friend called you that name."

Let me provide you a special note about anger. It's not helpful to say to a kid, or an adult for that matter, "I bet you're angry." Anger is not a primary core feeling. What I mean by this is that anger is a second level emotion covering up the primary unpleasant emotion of feeling that you are powerless/helpless. Anger sends a signal that an individual is finding a situation and/or another person out of their control. So, it's best to insert the words helpless or powerless into your guess when you suspect that someone is feeling angry.

Thus, it's best to say, "I bet you're feeling helpless...about what to do about the bully." For a list of words that describe pleasant and unpleasant feelings see the Appendix.

A llowing for validation does not mean that you are agreeing with the child. What it does do is allow for the child to see that you clearly get the dilemma from their perspective. If done correctly, the child at this point cannot say, "You don't understand me...you don't understand kids my age..." in an effort to manipulate to get his way. Moreover, if validation is done successfully, you have bonded with the child, the child understands that you are on his side, and the child gets that you are simply being a parent and doing what's right. It often encourages the child to say more.

Validation is confirming the legitimacy of the person's point of view. Validation starts with a statement such as: "It makes sense that" or "I can see how you would see", or "I completely agree that..." When validating do not disagree! Do not give your opinion. Do not say, "Yes, but..." For example, you could say, "It makes sense that you had a rough day since you got in trouble with the teacher, got called a name, and were hungry much of the day."

It is important to keep in mind that if you disagree or give your perspective before validating, then the person has a case that you don't get it, and all your hard work is for naught. Moreover, a "but" always invalidates every "yes" part previously mentioned, and therefore, is a useless response.

R eviewing options or setting limits with a child may not always be necessary. You must first decide if solving the problem is solely a child's decision, a joint child and parent decision, or a parent only responsibility.

Parents are clearly solely responsible for the safety and well being of a child. Children who are dangerous to themselves or others need to be directed with clear boundaries. Examples of parent-only decisions include determining curfew, monitoring appropriate age of certain media (TV shows, access to certain websites, electronic gaming), and stopping your child from bullying his siblings or peers. Examples of joint decisions include timing of homework, keeping up with chores, and selection of extracurricular activities. Examples of child only decisions include choice of friends, type of musical instrument to play, or what hobbies to engage in during their free time. Children should be allowed to make such decisions, provided of course, that their choices in people and activities are safe.

When children are given the freedom to make choices, and follow through with making solid and wise decisions, it is unnecessary for a parent to review options and set limits. But when children fail to follow through with their commitments and responsibilities, clearly, parents have the right to intervene. The key to implementing this final part of **H.E.A.R.** is to provide a limit or consequence that is natural for the problem in a firm and fair manner that does not excuse the behavior but also does not undo the compassion for the child's dilemma. It is often helpful to explore the options for resolution out loud with the child before making your final decision. At times, children show their buy-in to a resolution or limit during the option exploration phase—either verbally or nonverbally. Be looking for this agreement because it makes the whole H.E.A.R. process have a residual effect on the child.

When looking at options and setting limits, values and beliefs also come into play. What does the world tell us to do? What does the Bible suggest we do as parents?

So, for instance, when children inform us that they are anxious about things such as others' rejecting them, being away from parents while attending activities, or not being able to perform well in certain subjects in school, what do our life philosophies versus our spiritual frameworks guide us to do? Our society frequently sends a message that stress and unhappiness are bad. Therefore, parents tend to impulsively jump in and rescue children by giving advice or getting personally involved. However, this is often hovering over our children and undermining their chance to resolve the challenge autonomously and build their self confidence.

> **"We rejoice in our sufferings, knowing that suffering produces endurance, and endurance produces character, and character produces hope, and hope does not disappoint us, because God's love has been poured into our hearts through the Holy Spirit which has been given to us." Romans 5:3-5**

Even though we sometime struggle as parents with knowing the best way to support our children, just know that consistent, loving and positive support and reinforcement (training in the right things to do) forms a solid foundation for our children's self-confidence and decision-making skills—creating a win-win where both parents and children feel less anxious about options and outcomes.

CHAPTER
6

GOOD PARENTS FIGHT FAIR

Reckless words pierce like a sword, but the tongue of the wise brings healing. Proverbs 12:18

We now know that Hurricane Katrina, which was formed on August 23, 2005, was the costliest and one of the deadliest hurricanes in the history of the United States. It was the sixth strongest Atlantic hurricane on record to make landfall in the United States. The catastrophic effects it caused to the Gulf Coast stretched as far as 100 miles, including flooding 80% of the city of New Orleans and neighboring parishes for weeks, making it the deadliest U.S. hurricane since the 1928 Okeechobee Hurricane. It is believed that 1,836 people lost their lives in Hurricane Katrina and in the subsequent floods. The storm is estimated to have been responsible for $81.2 billion (2005 U.S. dollars) in damage. Criticism of the federal, state and local governments' reactions to the storm was widespread and resulted in an investigation by the United States Congress and the resignation of FEMA director, Michael Brown. There were 150,000 or more people, largely poor people with limited resources, still in New Orleans when the levees failed (see www.wikipedia.org/wiki/Hurricane_Katrina).

Many of the residents of New Orleans had no idea that their city was protected by such a fragile levee system. Others probably knew, but certainly didn't consider other living arrangements because they were satisfied with what they had. Others just considered New Orleans their home for life.

One of the lessons learned from the Katrina disaster is that there is a huge risk in living on an unstable foundation. Maybe you've never considered whether or not your family communication patterns are built upon a fragile levee system or a strong rock. But, we have been warned to set our home foundation on a solid rock so that when the storms come, and the winds blow and beat on our home, we will not fall because we are founded upon a rock.

Until people are persuaded or forced to sit in a therapist's office or 12-step program, they rarely think of the rules of engagement that they have used in dealing with their loved ones, whether that be their spouse, their child, their parents, or any other significant other. Generally, our engagements with others are automatic. Do you sometimes feel that your automatic cruise control gets you into trouble?

This past Sunday, my pastor's sermon was on "Making Disciples Here, There and Everywhere." A critical point of the sermon was that **"You cannot make what you cannot model!"** What are you modeling to others?

Let's consider for a moment your normal interactions with your family members. Peruse the sample of fair fighting rules below and notice how many you have violated in the past or are engaged in presently.

Lenore's Sample of Top 10 <u>Unfair</u> Fighting Moves

- **Putdowns**—Labeling, name calling, sarcastic remarks, etc.
- **Dominating**—Hitting, yelling, throwing things, etc.
- **Multiple Topics at a time**—Bringing-up unresolved issues from the past or multiple topics at once
- **"D" moves**—Demeaning, domineering or dogmatic insinuations or demands. Threatening divorce as the ultimate solution or to end the conversation
- **"You, you, you"**—Focusing mainly on what you want the other person to change or do
- **Fighting to the point where you forget the main topic or purpose**
- **Assuming**—Initially taking over and jumping to conclusions before gathering all the facts
- **Bringing-up others** such as in-laws or friends
- **Fighting for hours, all night, or for days.** This includes passive approaches like the silent treatment
- **"It's my way or the highway/no way!"**

One of the most common reactions I encounter from individuals after they read the top 10 unfair fighting moves is a humble snicker and a comment such as: "I do many of these...obviously I need to do better, but what in the world can I do?" We clearly never intend to be thoughtless and careless with others, but unintentionally we are.

Let's face it, when a problem occurs in our home, we generally react with quick and automatic responses. Many of our first responses are habitual and do not serve us well. We think we're being clear and making complete sense, but it's simply not so. Here's a simple example of the kinds of things we do. We might say to our child, "You are being a brat!" But, what are we really talking about and what are we asking them to do? Interestingly, one definition of "brat" is unpleasant and ill mannered. So, if we just say, "you are a brat," the person may not know exactly what you're referring to or how to change their behavior in the desired direction. But, if we say, "I'm finding you to be unpleasant and using poor manners … I'm not going to let you spend time with your friend until you stop arguing and do your chore," then the child knows exactly the behavior that we are addressing. The child will then have an idea what the problem is and what to do.

Hours and hours are spent on developing rules for sports. It seems like every year in football, the TV playback review rule is reevaluated to determine its benefit. **Have you ever truly spent significant time looking in-depth at your natural reactions to handling conflicts?** Would it not make sense to give this amount of focus to the rules of family engagements?

You cannot give away what you don't have! So, begin by learning the following list of top 10 fair fighting rules. Start by going down the list and checking-off which rules you are already naturally doing yourself when you are in conflict with others. Then identify any traits you need to work on. For any of the traits you need to work on: practice using those in different situations with other people, such as your spouse, coworkers, employees or your siblings. Practice one or two of them every day for one entire week. Then, once you get those down, move on to learning one or two more the next week. Do this for several weeks until you've acquired all of the fair fighting techniques. Even if you have to learn all 10 of the strategies, which you likely don't, the maximum amount of time

> "How can you say to your brother, Let me take the speck out of your eye, when there is the log in your own eye? You hypocrite, first take the log out of your own eye, and then you will see clearly to take the speck out of your brother's eye." Matthew 7:4-5

you would spend would be five weeks. After this exercise, you will be prepared to role model and mentor fair fighting for your kids.

Putting it All Together: Teach Your Child Fair Fighting Rules

- **No putdowns**—No name calling or labeling (things such as you're stupid, you're a jerk, you're a brat) no sarcastic remarks, no mimicking, etc. Ask the child to identify what the problem is and clarify what the person is requesting or what the person needs. Teach them not to judge the rightness or wrongness, but to first seek to understand.

- **No dominating or threatening**—No automatic responses, especially no hitting, no yelling, no throwing things, etc. Coach your child to be calm in his manner and concise in responses; to think before responding. Ask him to take time to think; to say, "Let me think about what you said and I will let you know later. "

- Sticking with **one topic at a time**—No bringing-up multiple issues at one time. Teach your child to focus on the problem at hand and not raise other issues.

- **No "D" words**—Coach your children to avoid being demeaning, domineering or dogmatic. Guide them not to intentionally hurt others with words. Have them state observations and use assertive exchange. For example, when they say a teammate "is a jerk," redirect them to consider telling their peer that "I won't train with you today if you curse at me again." Define assertiveness as a "win" for all parties involved, which can take time and creativity to determine. Encourage them to be lighthearted and humorous when appropriate to solve a problem; have them avoid being chronically serious.

- **No "you, you, you"**—Teach your children to cease saying, "you...you...you..." Have them take ownership for their own, and only their own, feelings. Have them use "I" statements. For example: coach them to say, "I got mad at...(tip: focus on the behavior)..." rather than "you made me mad when..." Prod them to set some effective boundaries by saying to others, "I request..."

- **No fighting without a statement of purpose—State your intention!** Educate them to say, "I'm doing this because... I need..." And, teach them to clarify the intention of the other party involved. Allow children to only fight if it's an important reason by teaching them not to major in a minor issue.

- **No assuming**—Educate the child to avoid being judgmental. Teach your children the difference between exercising good judgment and being judgmental. Have them make observations and focus on the facts and stay in the moment. Teach them about what it is to impulsively react without thinking about the facts and options beforehand.

- **No bringing-up others or past issues.** Teach your child that to carry resentment about a past issue makes for chronic irritability and vulnerability to over-responding.

- Timing is everything—**call time-outs** and pick your timing. Educate them that an effective time-out involves temporarily excusing oneself and agreeing to work on the issue again when all parties are ready.

- **No "it's my way or the highway"—Agree to Disagree!! Think of the best option or route to take at the moment.** Encourage them to have compassion for the other person's point of view. Have them learn to validate by first thinking to themselves, "It makes sense for the other person to feel this way because, from his perspective..."

To react without thought is to be impulsive and careless. We can be quickly reminded of the danger of acting on auto-pilot when we think of stories like the alleged house party rape incident involving members of the Duke University men's lacrosse team, that began in 2006. There were no heroes in this story and it was concluded that this was a case of the media and a legal prosecutor gone awry!

The details surrounding this debacle are covered in the April 23[rd,] 2007 edition of *Newsweek*. In sum, due to swift and false information about the incidents surrounding the Duke lacrosse party provided by District Attorney to the press, the press then labeled three lacrosse players as "hooligans." Immediately, Duke students rallied against the team in campus protests and shunned the three Lacrosse players. The three Duke students spent a year defending themselves and their reputations from the appalling accusations of kidnapping, assault and rape. But the three Duke lacrosse players, faced with the possibility of going to prison for 30 years (for a crime they did not commit!), were spared by the North Carolina Attorney General Roy Cooper. In the Spring of 2007, Cooper dropped the charges and declared that the three players were innocent, that no rape had taken place, that a "rogue prosecutor" had overreached and that, "in the rush to condemn, a community and a state lost the ability to see clearly."

Although this might be an extreme example of the dangers of acting rashly, and rushing to judgment before all of the facts are known, it demonstrates the same principles we must apply to if we are to achieve effective, fair conflict resolution in our various relationships – and in particular with our children. All of these relationships stand to benefit when we strive to be more thoughtful.

CHAPTER
7

DIRECTING CHANGE

"But, the wisdom from above is first pure, then peace-able, gentle, open to reason, full of mercy and good fruits, without uncertainty or insincerity." James 3:18

Waffle House! Oh yes, like many people in the South, I enjoy the Waffle House and my husband and son love to go there on Saturday mornings. It's actually become a tradition. In fact I can quote my husband's order now, "I'll have a triple scrambled with cheese on the side, medium bacon hold the weight, coffee with cream, and a tall glass of water." Oh yes, we are regulars and I'm not ashamed to admit it.

Well, not long ago, during one of our visits, I was sitting in a booth with my family and began having our standard dialogue with the waitress as she welcomed us: "How ya'll doin' today? Alright I hope—sure is busy today, do ya'll know whatcha havin'? Great! Let me have it…".

As she hustled around the Waffle House tending to her customers, she began talking out loud about her recent brawl with her teenage boy and noticed that we were interested in learning more, so she unloaded about his inappropriate behavior with his girlfriend. She proceeded to tell us how her son continuously tried to cover up his interaction with his girlfriend. She said that in the midst of all his clever cover-up, he did not fool her one bit, because, as she reported, "He done changed his story." In the midst of her pleasant twang, we witnessed how she stuck to the simple fact that he lied once, which had sent her on a mission, on which she soon discovered further deceptive use of the family computer and his indiscretion in using the popular social networking site "MySpace." She proudly reported her determination to steer him on the right track by limiting his interactions with his girlfriend and his use of the computer until he was proven more responsible.

On that day in that Waffle House, I turned to my son and said, "I like that woman!" Periodically, my son reenacts the exchange that occurred that day. It was one of those precious events that you don't forget. Since then, I have reflected on why that exchange was so impactful. Well, the answer is that in the complex world of city living, she was so refreshing. In her country charm, she made things so simple! You've heard the expression: "the plain and simple truth is…"

What's your general manner and approach when you direct your child? Do you have a set of basic principles

that you follow in parenting situations even when you are stressed, caught off-guard, or temperamental?

Determining how to change a child's negative behaviors into positive behaviors can be overwhelming. But, the key part of shaping and redirecting any child is learning how to talk with children. The process and manner you use is directly linked to the quality of the outcome. The following are the main foundational skills I recommend in order to effectively engage with your child.

Check to see how many of these behaviors you already use with your child.

When Shaping Children through Elementary Age

- ■ **Have high quality interactions.** Are you prepared to handle the matter simply and effectively? Are you clear and calm? Is the timing and place appropriate? Should you wait?
- ■ **Good eye contact.** Do you role model effective nonverbal communication? Do you do things such as bend down and engage the child in solid eye contact? Do you ask the child to look directly into your eyes? Teach that actions such as regular eye contact, nodding, or a "yes sir" or "yes ma'am" conveys messages such as listening, understanding, and respect.
- ■ **Be concise.** Mirror the child's level of communication and understanding. For example, with a toddler who is only saying two-word sentences, you may

want to keep your statement to, "No hit." Use the one-sentence or two-sentence rule with three to five year olds. State the main point early. For example, "Inside we walk, outside you may run." A five minute direct and simple discussion is better than a one hour argument because there is a better chance for the parent to demonstrate authentic power and control.

- ▣ **Tell the child what to do.** Being positive and telling a child what to do will keep you from yelling, feeling angry, or becoming out of control. For example say, "Keep your bottom on the slide with feet forward." Or say, "Keep your feet on the grass and wood chips."

- ▣ **Have the child repeat the directive.** Check the child's understanding of what he or she heard you say. Have the child recall what you said in their own words by asking something like, "Tell me what you think I said."

- ▣ **Use "I" statements.** This works especially well with kids who value their autonomy and resist orders. Rather than nagging or yelling something like, "Will you stop running and screaming?" Say, "Please do something for me ... I want you to walk and use an inside voice."

- ▣ **Use "first...then" or "when...then."** "First, pick up your clothes and place them in the drawers and then we will play the board game." "When you finish your math homework then you can go outside and play with the neighbors."

- ▣ **Feet first.** Instead of yelling from another room, walk into the room where your child is to observe what he or she is involved in at that moment. Then, during a natural break, have the child turn off the computer or turn it off yourself. Going to your child is a more fair approach, role models respectful behavior, and sends the message that you are serious.

◘ **Stick with choices you find are acceptable.** "Do you want to read first or do your science assignment first?" "Do you want to practice your cheers downstairs or outside?"

◘ **Give acceptable alternatives.** "You can't play ball in the house, but you can play in the garage, downstairs, or in the back yard." "You will be doing music this year, so would you like to try the guitar or the saxophone?"

◘ **Give the child time to vent feelings.** Many times just having a compassionate listener available will make all the difference and may save a tantrum or mental breakdown. Validate their experience and let them know you get their difficulty. Say, "You're frustrated because you're the oldest child and you have to set a good example by handling fighting with your words and not your fists."

◘ **Have the child complete the sentence.** Instead of, "Don't leave your clothes in the living room." Try, "Amy, your dirty clothes go where?" Or, "When you don't place your dirty clothes in the hamper who has to do that for you?" Or, "When mom picks up after you she feels…"

◘ **Firm, Fair endings.** Close discussions in a calm and confident manner, such as, "I will take your point into consideration, but for now it's time to end this discussion and do what we discussed."

Working with pre-teens and teens is a different ball game, isn't it? Think of it this way. Communication with young children is like Little League. Collegiate sports is more like relating to those pre-teens. And, sound communication and connection with teens is more like playing in the major leagues.

How many times have you heard from your teen some version of, "I'm tired of the lecture!"? Teens really don't respond if we're not on our game. They particularly shut down on parents who are long-winded, repetitive, and lecturing. So, here are some foundational tools to use with them:

The Foundational Principles of Effective Communication with Teens and Pre-Teens

- ◙ **Don't consistently lecture or nag.** Clarify the rules for the teen to follow or the consequences that will result only once or twice. There's no added benefit after one or two discussions in reiterating the information.

- ◙ **Give SMART requests.** Do you provide firm and smart requests? Smart requests are ones that are **S**pecific, **M**easurable, **A**chievable, **R**ealistic and **T**imely. As an example, rather than saying, "I want you to take out the trash this week." You say, "I expect for you to have the trash barrels out by the curb every Tuesday this month by 7pm."

▣ **Give only one or two consequences for every problem behavior.** There's an increased chance of things escalating and getting out of control when you give more than two consequences for a problem behavior. For example, your child lies about completing a homework assignment, and so you impulsively ground the child for two weeks. The teen becomes angry and argues and you give another week for the disrespect. The child continues to be argumentative and unapologetic so you add another week. Before long you've grounded the child for four weeks and you find yourself regretting what you've done because it's too harsh. Avoid mistakes like this by making the first consequence fit the crime and hold to it. As long as the child is making the correction by adhering to your requests, think twice before you get into a power struggle over a negative attitude. If you choose to ground your child, generally two weeks is sufficient. If you think a month is necessary, that's usually for something very serious and a time to consider seeking a professional consultation.

▣ **Coach.** It is the quality of the parent-teen interaction that is more important than the actual techniques used. Have you consistently assumed roles that are less effective than life coach; such as cop, EMT, judge, fisherman, doormat, sergeant, avoider, chauffer, friend, or maid?

◘ **Use the "carrot" and "stick" approach.** When disciplining, consider giving a consequence and a way to earn back privileges. For example, a child breaks curfew one night by coming home late and you decide that the "stick" that best fits the crime is to take away spending free time with their friends the next two weeks. At the same time, you give the child a "carrot" by allowing the child to attend the next week's school sponsored activities. You stipulate that as long as the child goes straight to the events and back home, is apologetic for the wrongdoing and maintains a good attitude throughout their punishment, then you will consider shortening the grounding.

◘ **Make sure your daily positive interactions are more frequent than your average daily negative interactions.** Are your verbal words and contact time more positive than negative? Children are not really bonded to their parents, or do not hire their parent as a mentor, manager or coach, unless there are more positive interactions than negative interactions on a daily basis. The ratio of positive to negative interactions needs to be at least 3 to 1.

◘ **Engage in positive talk.** How often do you find positive things to say about yourself, your teen or others? If you have a teen girl, how often do you find kind or positive things to say that have nothing to do with appearance. For boys, how often do you say positive things that have nothing to do with being cool, being a stud, or being successful?

- ▣ **Facilitate frequent, positive dinners together.** Your dinner experiences most closely correspond to the overall quality of your family interactions.
- ▣ **Build special times and special memories.** Do you have positive weekly, yearly and holiday rituals?
- ▣ **Encourage sharing of thoughts and feelings.** Are you curious about your teen's day-to-day life? Do you engage in conversations that are really about nothing just to maintain a bond with your teen? Do you give empathy and validation before explanations?
- ▣ **Know your buttons, and don't allow them to be pushed.** Don't allow your teen to manipulate you through attacking your weaknesses and vulnerabilities. For example, a teen who hasn't been diligent in preparing for the next season of his sport might say, "Dad, you don't exercise, so you don't have any business telling me how much I need to train right now." When your teen attempts to push your button you might say something like, "Nice try." Or you might say something like, "I'm not falling for that insult...do what you need to do to prepare and train adequately for the season..."
- ▣ **Stick to the rules.** You don't change the rules in the middle of an incident. You reevaluate in private at a later, calmer time. For example, a teen is on restriction from going out with friends due to a poor grade. The teen improves his behavior and almost meets the requirement but falls slightly short of the agreement and says, "I'm doing better, so can I please go out just tonight ... I know I'll do even better the next

time." One parent is softening and the other parent is not. The answer is you don't soften. You empathize, but nevertheless you stick with the consequence. The parents talk in private and if they do agree to change the rules, they don't change them until after this round of trouble is complete.

◼ **Let your teen make amends and then everyone move on.** Once your child has followed through with consequences for a wrongdoing and made acceptable correction for the problem behavior, require everyone in your family to move on. Do not bring up the issue in the future in an effort to pressure him to make a change. No saying, "Well, two years ago you did ... now you're doing ..." Not moving on breaks a child down through building shame. Shame is about a child believing they are bad and flawed. Ashamed children tend to be anxious, withdrawn, or resistant. They frequently get into power struggles with authority figures; either by passively avoiding adults or swinging into rebelliousness. Healthy guilt is the alternative to shame. Guilt involves the child realizing he did something wrong, and therefore he simply has to accept responsibility for the problem and see it as a problem that needs to be solved. As a parent, if you find yourself not being forgiving and not able to move on through either repeatedly raising an issue or ruminating over an issue, then you may need professional help.

With all people, no matter what the age, remember that every behavior, including misbehavior has a purpose and payoff. With misbehavior, observe the situation and guess what the child needs. After determining what your child is seeking to achieve, guide the child to acceptable alternative behaviors that have a similar payoff.

I've worked with many parents who actually know many parenting techniques, including reward systems, time-outs, and discipline options, but they don't work well with their children because their foundational parenting plan and approach is flawed. Their children have shut down on them and tuned them out. By adding the above tools to your toolbox, your children will be apt to respect your directives because you will create a balance of fairness, firmness and nurturance.

Over time, you can add more refined parenting techniques to your parenting toolbox. Examples of more specific parenting tools are the use of meaningful motivators and incentive programs, correct negotiation strategies during power struggles, shaping successive approximations of the desired behavior, selective ignoring, effective time-outs, and powerful praise. My favorite book providing a comprehensive, yet entertaining and easily read, overview of these strategies for children under age 12 is *How to Behave So Your Children Will Too!* (by Sal Severe, Ph.D.). The book I most recommend for your teens is *Parenting Your Out of Control Teenager* (by Scott Sells, Ph.D.).

CHAPTER
8

THE BLENDED FAMILY: BE CAREFUL BEFORE YOU "STEP"

"He who is greatest among you shall be your servant; whoever exalts himself will be humbled, and whoever humbles himself will be exalted." Matthew 23:11-12

One of the most confusing and humbling jobs to have in life must be the job of a stepparent. Even the name is confusing. Is this a step-up, a step-down, or what? Is the name referring to the idea of moving stepwise, or is it about staying one step removed?

Before you go any further, let me inform you that the information and strategies in this chapter are geared more for a stepparent where both of the biological parents are involved in the child's life. If you are a stepparent because the child's biological parent is deceased or has abandoned the child, then you are really the **parent**.

Stepparents observe the interactions between the biological parents and stepchildren from a birds-eye view. So, it's tempting to try and step-up and provide what he or she sees as a fresh, objective approach in an attempt to rescue their spouse from torn and tattered patterns. But, I say, be very careful before you step! Let's consider a few examples of challenging situations in blended families.

Example 1:

Sam is relieved to be "over" his divorce and newly married to Kylie. Sam's first marriage was very painful. He has no respect for his former wife, who developed a terrible alcohol problem after the birth of their first child. During the divorce process, Sam also discovered that his ex-wife had multiple affairs during their 8-year marriage. Sam saw his ex as self-indulgent and neglectful of his two children's needs, so the news of the extent of her out of control behavior did not come as a surprise to him. Sam's children, a boy and a girl, are now early elementary age.

Sam is confident in his choice of Kylie, as she's kind, attentive, caring, and a good role model for his children. Kylie is knowledgeable in how to manage children and parents, as she is a high school teacher with approximately 10 years of teaching experience in both public and private Christian schools.

Sam takes any chance he gets to encourage the children's negative feelings towards their biological mother in hopes that they will clearly see that her behavior is wrong and has serious negative consequences.

Sam has primary custody of the children and does not require his ex to keep consistent visitation with the children. When she does see them, she's what Sam calls the "Disneyland" parent who only does fun things with the children. Sam thinks this spoils the kids and doesn't give them a realistic picture of what real love from a mother really is. Sam figures the less time the kids have with her, the better. But, he realizes the children do need to see their mother.

Kylie is impressed with Sam's commitment to his children and his overall family values. Kylie is attracted to Sam for many reasons, including the fact that Sam is a strong individual who intends to do the right thing in the face of any adversity that comes his way. However, she knows that his resentment towards his ex and his badmouthing of his ex could be damaging to the children.

Example 2:

Mary's marriage ended after her husband had an affair and left the marriage. Mary is a determined, capable, optimistic and faithful woman. During consultation with her attorney during the divorce process, Mary knew that her alimony wouldn't last beyond a few years so she began developing a plan to be self-supporting within four to five years.

After the divorce, Mary was hopeful that her experience as a part-time interior decorating assistant could be turned into full-time self-employment. Temporarily, she increased her hours on the weekends at the retail store where she was currently working, which was generally a time when the children were with their father. Additionally, she returned to taking interior design certification courses during the week while her children, two middle school pre-teenage boys, were in school. This way, she was available to the boys every evening to take them to their after-school activities, make certain they did their homework, have dinner and spend some time with them.

Although Mary's ex was not a good husband, he was available to his children. He still spends as much time with the children as he can, including any time Mary is scheduled to work. The main problem Mary had with her ex's parenting style was that he let the kids do basically whatever they wanted at his home. He still does not monitor their TV viewing, video game usage, or cleanliness. But, when they return to her, the kids are generally good. It's just that they are argumentative and uncooperative when asked to take the initiative to pick-up after themselves, when reminded to view only age-appropriate movies, or when told to play games a reasonable amount of time.

Much of the time Mary is too tired to fight the boys over helping around the house and being reasonable with their choices. Thus, the home is a wreck, the children are under-achieving in school, and her children are perceived as being somewhat disrespectful by others.

Mary is now in the second year beyond her divorce and she is engaged to Eric. Eric is confident that he and Mary are right for each other. Eric is impressed with Mary and the whole blended family situation. He's seen other divorce situations that haven't been handled so maturely and wisely.

However, he recognizes that he has some differences in how he likes the home kept and he sees how the children can be unruly at times. Eric believes his need for organization and structure will be very helpful in helping the boys become better-rounded in their life. He figures that they can simply work these challenges out as they arise.

Example 3:

Greg has been a single father since age 18. His marriage lasted only six months before he realized he was making a big mistake committing to something so long-term with another unstable person. The divorce was a rude awakening for him and he soon returned to moving on with his life in a positive direction. He quickly enrolled in college and completed his Business Management Bachelor's degree.

Greg is now 29 and ready to marry Helen, who is a competent and soft spoken woman who's never been married and has no children. Helen is a successful CPA and he has a stable management position in the retail industry. Greg and Helen have discussed having a child of their own. His children are now 11 and 10.

The mother of Greg's children is now a hard-working administrative assistant. Her salary is in the $30,000 range and many times she has difficulty making ends meet. Greg realizes that she clearly needs his child support and extra financial help to cover expenses for the children, such as children's sports activities, orthodontics, music lessons, etc., which he has always consistently provided. Thus, there is relatively low tension in their co-parenting.

Helen sees Greg as very kind and a good balance to her more intellectual style. However, she does believe that he sometimes allows his ex-wife to take advantage of him. Helen has observed that regularly, and desperately, his ex requests extra assistance from him when she's simply been less than careful with the monthly child support she receives. Helen believes that the ex has used the child support for her own expenses, not just expenses related to the children. Helen is thinking that over time she can influence Greg to not be so easily influenced and manipulated by his ex.

Which one of these examples is most similar to your situation?

If you are, or about to be, a stepparent like Kylie, Eric and Helen, then you are now in the business of remodeling. It is, however, a special type of remodeling, called family remodeling. What you are challenged with is assisting in the cleanup of the wreckage that the divorce has created for your stepchildren, without creating more unnecessary hardship for them, yourself, and your new marriage. To minimize more hardship for everyone, there are some important steps to take.

The first step to take when developing your stepparenting plan is to **be thoughtful about matters of the "heart"**.

The first matter of the heart is that you must be very clear and brutally honest with yourself about your intentions in this marriage and with each stepchild. Ask yourself the following:

- What will this marriage offer me?
- What payoffs do I expect will come from being a stepparent?
- How is stepparenting in a blended family system different from parenting in an intact family?

Secondly, you must be extremely patient and considerate about the stages of grief that every child struggles with after their trauma with divorce and separation from a biological parent. Most counselors say that it takes an average of two years for an individual to go through grief after a significant loss of any kind, whether that is a move to a new location, a new school, a new job, or a new significant circumstance of any kind.

The phases of grief of a child are similar to that of an adult (shock, denial, bargaining, anger, depression, and eventually resolution/acceptance), but their understanding is tremendously impacted by their developmental level, personality and individual circumstances. You can begin by understanding how the child is interpreting and managing her loss by being a solid emotion coach, which is covered in chapter 5 of this book. But, there is no replacement for consulting with a professional counselor in the area of grief and loss if one is to truly have compassion for what the child is experiencing.

The third matter of heart is to always have a spirit of fairness about you. Everyone must win at some level. Go for win-win in every situation; a win for you and a win for each of them. This will require true compassion, especially if the children involved seem amiable and compliant. Some mistake children's compliance as acceptance of circumstances and a sign that a child is doing well. Just because a child is quiet or cooperative about matters, including a dating parent, a move, or other life changes, does not mean he completely embraces what's happening. An agreeable or stoic nature is often due to a child feeling helpless to change what's happening around him, feeling fearful of disappointing his main custodial parent, being unskilled to acknowledge his inner hurts, and/or believing he is powerless to assert what he really wants. And don't mistake an angry, noncompliant child for not doing well. She may simply be in the angry phase of the expected grief process, and therefore, in need of more time to go through her adjustment to the losses she has endured.

Finally, be mindful that one thing that never seems to get easy for kids, no matter what age and no matter what they say, is transitioning from Mom to Dad and vice versa. It's a top complaint of kids who come to therapy, whether or not it's the reason they came to therapy in the first place. Given that transitioning the child amongst parents can be so rough on the parents, it's easy to fall into the trap, consciously or accidentally, of having the exchange be more about what's best for the parent.

Exchanging children is one of those consequences of divorce that is really more of a burden on kids than on parents. The kids are the ones who have to manage this strain over and over again. The closest analogy to their situation is that of a traveling salesperson. Shuffling back and forth between parents is a necessary evil. For some kids it's the first time that they have to really come to terms with the fact that we don't live in a world that's always fair. The children didn't cause the divorce, but yet they're the ones who have to accept their complex living arrangements. So, make these transitions as free of conflict as possible and about what's best for the children. Occasionally, you may even want to tell your children that you realize that this is something they must do and give them a simple, authentic "thank you." Moreover, this is a situation where it's appropriate to ask the children for feedback about what would make their transitions easier, such as obtaining information about what clothing to have on hand to help reduce or eliminate the need for packing, what school items to have available, what type of a work space would help them study, etc.

Keep in mind that when dealing with matters of the heart, compassion for a child's losses and hurts can be exhibited without excusing bad behavior. Grieving and enduring loss is never an excuse for problem behavior. For example, awakening upset about a divorce is not an excuse to avoid school. At times like this, it's important to quickly acknowledge the dilemma and aid a child in agreeing to discuss the pain in an acceptable fashion and an appropriate time after school.

To make the child's life more manageable it's also helpful to outline household standards that are fair and expected for children to follow. Therefore, the second step to take as a stepparent is to **discuss household rules and family rituals** you and your spouse believe are necessary to incorporate in your everyday life, which will uphold a healthy functioning environment for all family members. To begin this exercise, have each of you independently come up with a list of your top 10 daily family rules and rituals before discussing the list together. It may take some time to reach an agreement and you may have to consult with a counselor if this process is too difficult or not progressing.

After reaching an agreement as a couple about family rules, it's important for the biological parent to first discuss the expectations with his biological children and then to direct and remind the children to follow the family rituals and guidelines. If the children resist the new expectations, it's important for the biological parent to address the resistance and seek help if necessary. It's not the job of the stepparent to intervene and take over this process. The job of the stepparent is to juggle encouraging their spouse, waiting patiently while the spouse is working this out, and holding the spouse accountable so as to not drop this process if it becomes challenging. This is where things can get tricky or even downright ugly.

Some folks persist through the difficult task of developing household guidelines and expectations assuming many roles, including becoming the family therapist who tries to analyze and persuade their spouse, or the rescuer who tries to control the destination of the family. If these aforementioned strategies fail, the individual may give up, disengage, or attempt to avoid the situation altogether. Other people ultimately find this task daunting and just resign themselves to going along for the ride; leaving the family the dubious task of resorting to whatever it's going to become.

It's important not to fall into such traps as the "rescuer", "controller," "disengager," or "enabler" with your loved one. For a reminder of effective, fair negotiation strategies and qualities of healthy families, refer to the earlier chapters of this book.

Also, if you are serious about creating a healthy blended family climate, without compromising your marriage, it's essential to understand the most correct role to assume for the stepchildren. Thus, the third move to make as a stepparent is to step back for a few moments and consider that **the correct role of a stepparent is most similar to the role of an Aunt or Uncle.**

The upside of being an honored Aunt or Uncle is the revered yet casual relationship we get to enjoy with our nephews and nieces. If we're smart as Aunts and Uncles, we don't want to lose our special position by nagging or lecturing. Furthermore, we remember that this is our sibling's child, so we must assume the role of being a wise mentor that honors the child's well-being and safety as needed.

As a stepparent, if you think of your role as the involved and esteemed Aunt or Uncle, you will likely avoid power struggles and serve as a key person in the child's life. By taking a step-down from the biological parents, you will find yourself in fewer entanglements with ex-husbands or ex-wives, and serve as an involved support to your spouse.

Moreover, do not resort to being the cool friend rather that the enjoyable, effective stepparent. Have clear boundaries. You have probably observed many school teachers who are revered by students because they are enjoyable yet healthy mentors. They're looked up to because students feel that these adults "get it;" these teachers apparently empathize with kids, while equally guiding them through their trials and tribulations. Teachers do not support self-destruction or self-harm, and the children know this. The children know that they are too important for a mentor to stand by and aid in self-destructive behavior. Humans crave mentors like teachers, aunts, and uncles. So, I hope you are up to the challenge of working into this type of special role.

The last considerations in developing your foundational stepparenting plan are really warnings about **certain snares to avoid**. First, understand that excessive fighting between the biological parents, whether that be directly between them or indirectly (e.g. when a parent isn't present, bad-mouthing that parent in front of the child by labeling the parent as fundamentally flawed in some way such as irresponsible and unreliable), is correlated with lower self-worth and academic underachievement in children. One reason for this is that kids see their parents as an extention of themselves. For example, children can think that if their parent is "bad" that somehow they are flawed too. In these situations, the child lives not only in the chronic hurt that comes from being separated from a parent but the lethargy of shame. Living in such disgrace, distracts a person and bogs them down leaving less motivation and energy. To a child, two days is a long time, to a pre-teen two weeks is a long time, and to a teen two months is a long time. You certainly don't want a child to live in a cloud of shame for months and months. So, as a stepparent don't tolerate bad-mouthing in your home.

Second, psychological experts believe that children are best parented by their two biological who work in harmony as co-parents. However, this is assuming that the biological parents are generally healthy (e.g. not abusive, not actively using drugs, not abusing alcohol, etc.). It is important that the biological parents be the father and mother figures, but if this is impossible due to a biological parent being impaired, it is important to reach-out to professional counselors. The counselor will help you figure out the appropriate role for yourself to serve with the children and the appropriate type of interactions to support—amount of and locations of— between the children and the impaired biological parent.

Further snares to avoid are best described by Thomas Whiteman, who is a leading expert in the field of divorce, blended family and single parent support. As found in Whiteman's workbook, *The Fresh Start Single Parenting Workbook,* every adult helping manage a blended family should be aware of the following:

- Statistically, only 40 percent of single dads see their children at all two years after the breakup. The reasons for this include the fact that some men find losing their wife and children as "too painful" to endure, some give up because they feel they have no control or influence anymore, and others feel "replaced" or "no longer needed" especially if a new man is involved with their ex-wife.

- Without a positive father figure in their life, girls have a tendency toward sexual identity problems, may become promiscuous to gain attention from men, may marry someone who parents them, or may have difficulty in committed relationships. Sons, on the other hand, may experience a much lower self-image, may question their own masculinity, may have a greater likelihood of juvenile delinquency, or may fall into a cycle of chronic underachievement or underemployment.

• Some biological parents can become discredited as a role model or authority figure by their children if they have not represented the standards that children want to live by when they grow up. Choices that overburden kids with adult responsibilities (excessive chores, caring for younger siblings, having irresponsible babysitters out of desperation, turning the child into a "latchkey" kid, witnessing transitory dating relationships) leave them angry and disillusioned about adults. Thus, many of these kids are disrespectful of authority figures.

In sum, it is important to step carefully and thoughtfully as a stepparent. Realize that children of divorce need consistent follow-through from a stepparent who's truly interested in their well being and their complex life. For many of these children, it takes an effective, consistently loving stepparent to rebuild their sense that adults can be dependable. They need a stepparent to encourage and support co-parenting in a harmonious manner. They need stepparents to understand that they really do need a father figure, especially their biological father. And, they need support and validation of their grief. This will go a long way for the child in terms of rebuilding themselves, embracing their new life circumstances, and functioning positively in their new blended family.

CHAPTER
9

FINAL THOUGHTS

"The eye is the lamp of the body. So, if your eye is sound, your whole body will be full of light." Matthew 6:22

It's been between 18° and 28° F lately here in Atlanta. This bitter cold is strange for this area of the country, but not so unlike those cold winter mornings in Colorado where I grew up. I can remember my father getting up each morning to care for our family horses before leaving for work—facing winter elements much more severe than we typically have in the Southeast. My father had to navigate frequently through both ice and snow as he traveled country roads on his way to the horse stables and then onto Denver where his office was located. Year after year, my Dad made these kinds of sacrifices for us, his children, always doing his best.

Just like my mother and father, we parents have chosen to have children. Don't our children deserve the best that we can offer them? We know that our job is not to simply accessorize them, but to equip them. Unfortunately, the world doesn't teach what's at the heart of a quality parent-child relationship.

Hopefully, after reading this book, you have identified the tools needed to build a rock solid parenting plan — many of which you probably already possess. The plan has focused largely on "building" yourself, so that you can assist your family in dealing with life's challenges effectively. And, the plan has been about giving you proper perspective and instruction about how to improve your parenting style, your family climate, your conflict resolution skills, and your ability to bond with and coach your child.

But, I caution you that your new knowledge may come at a price. Very few things split neighbors, friends and families more quickly than differences in parenting styles. You may find yourself disconnected from others in your community who don't share these rock solid parenting principles. It's simply another trickery of evil forces to split people. Remember, there is wisdom in being patient and waiting on others to solicit your advice and help. And, even when others do ask for your assistance, it is always wise to proceed carefully and thoughtfully.

Know that people are people, and it's not a matter of "if" kids will make mistakes, it's a matter of "when". No one makes it through this life without making a few bad choices and without having a few "chunks of flesh" taken out of them. I have observed that if a person with a solid foundation strays off-track, he or she tends to gravitate back to their roots once the stormy period has passed. People tend to be consistent with behaviors that they have demonstrated in the past. But, as we have learned, there are certainly positive steps we can take to help our children make the consistently sound decisions that keep them from straying in the first place.

You might be wondering: *"How will I know if I have a solid parenting plan in place for my children?"* Since 1989, The Search Institute has surveyed over two million youth across the United States and Canada. These researchers have developed what they call the "40 Developmental Assets", which are the positive experiences and personal qualities that young people need in order to grow up healthy. The 40 assets were grouped into the following types of categories (see www.search-institute.org/assets/):

- External support – such as positive family communication, other caring adult relationships, caring school climate, parent involvement
- External boundaries and expectations – such as clear family/school/neighborhood boundaries and positive peer influence
- Constructive use of time – such as creative activities, involvement in youth programs, involvement in religious community, and quality time at home
- Internal assets - positive values (e.g. as integrity, honest, caring, responsibility, restraint), commitment to learning, social competencies, and positive self-identity

Based on the Search Institute's 2003 survey of nearly 150,000 6th - 12th grade youth, they suggested that a child with only 50% or less of the developmental assets has a 26-45% risk of problems with alcohol use, a 38-62% chance of engaging in violence, an 18-38% chance of illicit drug use, and 23%-34% chance of sexual acting out. Moreover, they reported that the average young person surveyed in the U.S. experiences only 19 of the 40 assets. Apparently, 59% of the young people surveyed have 20 or fewer of the assets. For additional information about the 2003 survey findings, please see their website (see www.search-institute.org/research/assets/assetpower.html). Clearly, there is a correlation between the quality of decisions being made by young people, and the presence (or absence) of a strong, healthy developmental foundation, as provided by parents and other authority figures.

Everybody makes mistakes in life, but it is far better that these mistakes be simply accidents rather than the avoidable consequences of a negligent parenting plan. With the rock solid parenting plan, you begin to build the foundation of what is necessary for fostering a healthy atmosphere, one that focuses on constant and consistent support for our children. The rock solid parenting plan is about fine tuning:

- An authoritative parenting style where kids are provided with loving yet firm support and opportunities to develop core life skills.
- A positive family climate that allows children to have time at home with high quality interaction, which forms their character and relational skills.

- A quality spiritual life, which empowers children with perspective and a solid community that supports healthy habits and values.
- Solid life coaching that encourages children to embrace their parent as their mentor, while at the same time, these well coached children will be developing emotional intelligence.
- Fair and effective communication and conflict resolution that serves as a training ground and solid example of healthy relations.

Parenting children takes great passion, and it can quickly expose our inadequacies. Refining our parenting skills and utilizing a sound parenting plan minimizes our parental weaknesses, which is a gift not only to the child, but also to us because it helps complete us. We experience internal peace and a greater sense of focus, not only in our parent-child relationships, but in other areas of our lives as well when we're parenting effectively.

Where is your focus, and your passion? Where are your priorities? Are you leading a balanced life or are you excessively distracted about your career, your body, or some other self-absorbed passion?

Through my practice, I have witnessed some parents that lack authentic passion for parenting—as evidenced by things such as spending only a token amount of time with their children and family, or having their family members continually participate in selfish adult activities that are really not family preferred activities. Others still may ride on the coattails of the other parent. When parents are so self-absorbed, there is something terribly wrong. These parents likely need the other parent to place a firm boundary of no toler-ance for this negligence. I recommend an immediate consult with a professional psychologist or licensed professional counselor to indentify the problems that are preventing these parents from being meaningfully connected to their children.

> "I therefore, a prisoner for the Lord, beg you to lead a life worthy of the calling to which you have been called, with all lowliness and meek-ness, with patience, forbearing one another in love, eager to main-tain the unity of the Spirit in the bond of peace." Ephesians 4:13

Each and every week, I evaluate if I'm "building" the right parenting environment. This means, I literally inspect my parenting plan at least 52 times a year. This might sound like a lot, but really, I'm only doing what most of us do every single day—taking a look at myself in the mirror and asking: *"What am I going to do today?"*

Pausing a minimum of one time per week to evaluate if your current actions are truly a reflection of your overall parenting plan is not only a small investment in the success of our parenting strategies, it's exactly the kind of consistent behavior we are asking THEM to demonstrate, and the type of consistent devotion our children deserve.

And remember, as suggested earlier, there is a simple solution for addressing any areas of your parenting plan that need more work upon inspection. Indentify the aspects that are lacking, and practice one or two of them every day for a week. Once the new, more desired behaviors become habitual, move on to any other areas that need work the following week.

This method of identifying and addressing opportunities for improvement has been invaluable for me, and I am confident it can also be an effective method of change for you. In this way, you are constantly checking and adjusting your parenting focus, keeping an eye on your overall plan, and keeping in mind these essential questions:

- **B**—Am I using the <u>best parenting style</u>?
- **U**—Do I <u>understand the type of family climate</u> currently operating in my family? Right now, is it healthy or detrimental? Do I need to make some changes?
- **I** —Have I <u>involved my children in quality spiritual support</u> and discussions?
- **L**—Am I utilizing <u>life coaching</u>?
- **D**—Am I <u>directing change effectively</u> and fighting fairly?

By applying the concepts outlined in this book, we as parents have the opportunity to maximize the strength and quality of the relationships we build with our children. And whether it's the loving, respectful gaze of our children, or just a more confident and self-assured reflection looking back at us from the mirror, we are also more likely to be pleased with the results we see.

REFERENCES

Barna, G. 2003. *Transforming children into spiritual champions: Why children should be your church's #1 priority.* Ventura, California: Regal Books.

Evans, R. 2004. *Family matters: How schools can cope with the crisis in childrearing.* San Francisco: John Wiley & Sons.

Goleman, D. (1995). *Emotional intelligence: Why it can matter more than IQ.* New York: Bantam Books.

Gottman, J. 1997. *Raising an emotionally intelligent child: The heart of parenting.* New York: Fireside.

Hathaway, W.I. & Pargament, K.I. (1990). Intrinsic religiousness, religious coping, and psychosocial competence: A covariance structure. *Journal for the Scientific Study of Religion, 29*(4), 423-442.

Koenig, H.G., Pargament, K.I., & Nielsen, J. (1998). Religious coping and health status in medically ill hospitalized older adults. *The Journal of Nervous and Mental Disease, 186*(9), 513-521.

McGraw, P.C. 2004. *Family first.* New York: Free Press.

Overton, W.B. (2000). *From me—to you: The role of accurate and effective communication in building satisfying and fulfilling relationships that enrich all of life.* Alcoa,TN: Author (posthumously).

Pargament, K.I., Ensing, D.S., Falgout, K., Olsen, H., Reilly, B., Van Haitsma, K.V., et al. (1990). God help me (I): Religious coping efforts as predictors of the outcomes to significant negative life events. *American Journal of Community Psychololgy, 18*(6), 793-824.

Pargament, K.I., Kennell, J., Hathaway, W., Grevengoed, N., Newman, J., & Jones, W. (1988). Religion and the problem-solving process: Three styles of coping. *Journal for the Scientific Study of Religion, 27,* 90-104.

Pargament, K.I., Smith, B.W., Koenig, H.G., & Perez, L. (1998). Patterns of positive and negative religious coping with major life stressors. *Journal for the Scientific Study of Religion, 37*(4), 710-724.

Sells, S.P. (2001). *Parenting your out-of-control teenager: 7 steps to reestablish authority and reclaim love.* New York: St. Martin's Griffin.

Severe, S. 1999. *How to behave so your children will, too!* Tempe, AZ: Greentree Publishing.

Wenner, M. (2007, April 24). Study: Religion is Good for Kids. *LiveScience.* Retrieved January 30, 2008, from http://www.livescience.com/health/070424_religion_kids.html

Whiteman, T.W. (1993). *The fresh start single parenting workbook.* Nashville, TN: Thomas Nelson Publishers.

Whiteman, T.W. (2001). *Helping your kids survive your divorce.* Grand Rapids, MI: Baker Publishing Group.

ABOUT THE AUTHOR

Dr. Lenore Doster is a Licensed Psychologist practicing in Atlanta, Georgia. She currently provides psychotherapy for adults, teens, and children in individual and family therapy. Her practice includes spiritual integration into the recovery process and her specialties include: life transitions across the life span, parenting, young adult development, eating disorders, chronic and severe mental illness, stress management and anger management.

Lenore's clinical background includes providing psychological services at The Summit Counseling Center, where she has been a therapist since the Fall of 2003, the Atlanta Center for Eating Disorders, and Grady Memorial Adult Day Treatment Center. She completed her American Psychological Association Accredited Doctoral Internship at Philhaven Psychiatric Hospital, a non-profit Mennonite affiliated facility in Pennsylvania. While at Philhaven, she received specialized training in spiritual integration into psychological practice and in intensive therapy for married couples in crisis.

Prior to being a psychologist, Lenore was in higher education administration for over 7 years. She specialized in student affairs and worked for the Georgia Institute of Technology and The Ohio State University in housing administration.

Lenore's educational background includes: a Bachelor's degree in Psychology from Colorado State University, a Master's degree in Higher Education Administration & Student Affairs from The Ohio State University, a Master's degree in Clinical Psychology from the Georgia School of Professional Psychology, and a Doctorate of Psychology degree from Argosy University.

Lenore's special interest in working with parents from a biblical perspective began due to her own family and spiritual experiences. Lenore was raised in a large Catholic family in Castle Rock, Colorado. She was a member of Peachtree Christian Church, Disciples of Christ, from 1990 – 2002; served there as a Deacon and was active in various ministries including children's ministry and church growth. She has been married since 1991. She is a mom and a member of Mount Pisgah United Methodist Church located in Alpharetta, Georgia.

APPENDIX

Feelings

Positive Feelings		Negative Feelings	
Adaptable	Hardy	Abandoned	Hurt
Adept	Hopeful	Aggravated	Ignored
Affectionate	Honorable	Alienated	Inadequate
Alive	Humorous	Alone	Incompetent
Altruistic	Joyful	Apprehensive	Indecisive
Amused	Loveable	Ashamed	Ineffective
Assured	Loved	Awkward	Inferior
Beautiful	Loving	Befuddled	Inhibited
Benevolent	Loyal	Bitter	Insecure

Positive Feelings		Negative Feelings	
Brilliant	Magnificent	Bored	Irritated
Calm	Mighty	Broken	Isolated
Capable	Noble	Burned	Jealous
Caring	Optimistic	Contempt	Lonely
Cheerful	Overjoyed	Crippled	Melancholy
Cherished	Passionate	Crushed	Miserable
Comfortable	Patient	Defeated	Misunderstood
Competent	Peaceful	Dejected	Muddled
Confident	Playful	Despairing	Needy
Considerate	Pleased	Desperate	Outraged
Content	Powerful	Devastated	Overwhelmed
Courageous	Quiet	Disappointed	Panicky
Courteous	Reasonable	Discouraged	Powerless
Curious	Receptive	Disgusted	Puny
Delighted	Relaxed	Distrustful	Recoiling
Desirable	Relieved	Exasperated	Sickened

Positive Feelings		Negative Feelings	
Eager	Respected	Exposed	Spiteful
Ecstatic	Safe	Fearful	Timid
Excited	Satisfied	Flustered	Touchy
Forgiving	Self-reliant	Foolish	Trapped
Friendly	Sharp	Frantic	Trivial
Fulfilled	Silly	Frustrated	Troubled
Generous	Skillful	Furious	Unappreciated
Glad	Strong	Guilty	Unattractive
Giving	Supportive	Hateful	Uncertain
Good	Sympathetic	Helpless	Uncomfortable
Gracious	Tender	Hopeless	Uneasy
Grand	Thrilled	Horrified	Unfulfilled
Grateful	Unique	Hostile	Unsound
Great	Unselfish	Humiliated	Vulnerable

CPSIA information can be obtained at www.ICGtesting.com
234096LV00001B/16/P